Up You MIGHTY Race

An Introduction to Marcus Garvey

handwritten: WYATT FROM: GRANDAD 2018

Adrian Mandara Ph.D.

LMH PUBLISHING LIMITED

Edited by: K. Sean Harris
Illustrations: Courtney Robinson
Cover Design: Sanya Dockery
Book Design, Layout & Typeset: Sanya Dockery
Photographs of National Heroes' Park & Liberty Hall: Tony Patel

Published by: LMH Publishing Ltd.
Suite 10-11
Sagicor Industrial Park
7 Norman Road
Kingston C.S.O, Jamaica
Tel: 876-938-0005
Fax: 876-759-8752
Email: lmhbookpublishing@cwjamaica.com
Website: www.lmhpublishing.com

Printed in China

ISBN: 978-976-8245-18-2

NATIONAL LIBRARY OF JAMAICA CATALOGUING-IN-PUBLICATION DATA

Mandara, Adrian
    Up you mighty race / Adrian Mandara

    p. : ill. ; cm.

ISBN 978-976-8245-18-2 (pbk)

1. Garvey, Marcus, 1887-1940
I. Title

920   dc 23

Contents

Dedication

To the many well-thinking Jamaicans,

tired of the struggle,

But who still dream the dream

and still keep faith.

"My race is mine and I belong to it. It climbs with me and I shall climb with it. My pride is mine and I shall surely honour it. It is the height on which I daily sit."

Marcus Garvey

The Indispensable Weekly
The Voice of the Awakened Negro

Negro World

Reaching the Mass of Negroes
The Best Advertising Medium

A Newspaper Devoted Solely to the Interests of the Negro Race

VOL. XXI. No. 19   NEW YORK, SATURDAY, DECEMBER 18, 1926   PRICE: FIVE CENTS IN GREATER NEW YORK TEN CENTS ELSEWHERE IN THE U. S. A. TEN CENTS IN FOREIGN COUNTRIES

Hundreds of Thousands, White and Black, Dissatisfied At the Imprisonment of Marcus Garvey, Says Prominent White Paper

The following editorial, headed "A Tribute to Garvey," appeared in the Buffalo Evening Times (White) of Thursday, December 2, 1926. In this article the Times reiterates its belief that the Hon. Marcus Garvey was the victim of a trick statute and that he was guilty of no conscious wrong in the promotion of the movement which he espoused:

A TRIBUTE TO GARVEY

We have on more than one occasion pointed out that a vast number of white people and hundreds of thousands of black people in this country regard with a sense of regret and dissatisfaction the manner in which Marcus A. Garvey, the Negro leader of the "Back to Africa" movement for his people, was sent to the Atlanta Penitentiary for a period of five years. The method of his conviction was via the well worn "using the mails to defraud" route. This statute is reputed to be a means of "getting" anyone it is the purpose to "get," when every other legalistic expedient fails.

His trial raises the ethical if not the legal question as to whether he was a properly qualified protector of his own rights. He acted as his own attorney, called himself as witness, asked and answered questions in the dual capacity of witness and attorney, and so fumbled his case as to excite mingled amusement, derision, amazement, and in all probability consequent prejudices on the part of the jury which brought in a verdict of conviction.

Now on the front page of the New York Times Book Review for November 21, 1926, Evans Clark, in discussing Professor Jerome Dowd's book on "The Negro in American Life," makes this passing reference to the Garvey movement:

"Mr. Dowd reviews, somewhat more briefly, other proposals for the solution of the Negro problem. Colonization he dismisses as inconceivable, although he does go out of his way to say that the Garvey movement is 'a matter of serious import, in every respect creditable to its leader and to all who are backing it'."

This is no idle tribute. Mr. Dowd is Professor of Sociology in the University of Oklahoma. A native of South Carolina, he has had opportunity to study the colored race during the years of his childhood, youth and manhood; and no one has delved more conscientiously into the problems which confront the Inter-racial Congress than Mr. Dowd. He is neither a theorist nor a partisan in the discussion of a question which looms large for the good or ill of future years. Probably no man in the country has a calmer viewpoint or more comprehensive knowledge as regards this whole subject. Mr. Clark says of him:

"For twenty years Mr. Dowd has given himself to an investigation of the Negro problem. Convinced that an understanding of the question 'would not be possible without a study of the Negro in his original habitats and in regions to which he had been transplanted,' Mr. Dowd has dug deep into Negro history and written several volumes on the subject. In addition he has found it necessary 'to make excursions into biology, anthropology, eugenics and psychology, all of which sciences have made valuable contributions to our understanding of racial problems'."

This is the man who does not hesitate to speak in the kindliest fashion of Marcus Garvey, even though the latter is at the moment in the Atlanta Penitentiary. It reminds one of the brave action of Roald Amundsen in standing by Dr. Cook. But it has this difference, that Cook and Amundsen have been and are personal friends, while Professor Dowd as a South Carolinian could not by any possibility have had any such intimate association with the "Back to Africa" leader. His outspoken tribute is therefore all the more significant, and it bears out the opinions frequently expressed in this paper. We have never believed, and we do not believe now, that Marcus Garvey was guilty of any conscious wrong in the promotion of a movement which he espoused as the only means, as he saw it, of social emancipation and industrial progress for his race.

Courtesy of the National Library of Jamaica

Preface

- Black consciousness
- Black pride
- Black economic empowerment
- Black unity
- Self-confidence
- Solidarity of all black people
- Back-to-Africa Movement

All of the above mentioned are ideas that Marcus Mosiah Garvey advocated. He believed that Negroes were oppressed and seemed powerless to help themselves. This state of affairs he wished to change. He exhorted Negroes to become conscious, be self-confident, have pride in self and be competent in whatever field of endeavour they chose.

To appreciate Marcus Garvey, his vision and philosophy, it is necessary to understand his life and the challenges he faced and the many things he tried to do. His themes still resonate even today not only in Jamaica but throughout the Negro diaspora.

Jamaica's first National Hero, the Right Excellent Marcus Mosiah Garvey, remains a very timely and important figure, one that all Jamaican children should be familiar with. He certainly underpins Jamaica's civics and politics.

*The monument to the Right Excellent Marcus Mosiah Garvey, National Hero,
located at National Heroes' Park.*

The Right Excellent Marcus Mosiah Garvey

Marcus Mosiah Garvey, Jr., was born August 17, 1887 in St. Ann's Bay, Jamaica, West Indies. His parents were Marcus Mosiah Garvey, Sr. and Sarah Garvey.

Marcus Garvey was a man with many talents: journalist, publisher, businessman and orator, well-known for Black Nationalism, Black economic development and Pan-Africanism.

He was married twice - the first marriage was to Amy Ashwood in 1919 but this did not last and they were divorced in 1922. Garvey's second marriage was to Amy Jacques in 1922 who gave him two sons, Marcus Mosiah Garvey III and Julius Garvey. This was a happier relationship for Garvey.

Marcus Mosiah Garvey, Jr. died June 10, 1940 in London, England. He was made a National Hero of Jamaica in 1964.

Liberty Hall was the Kingston division of the U.N.I.A. and A.C.L. organisation. It housed the office of Marcus Garvey, a restaurant, a bank and other businesses.

The Early Years

Marcus Mosiah Garvey, Jr. was born August 17, 1887 in St. Ann's Bay in the parish of St. Ann in Jamaica, West Indies.

His father was Marcus Garvey, Sr., a mason, and his mother, Sarah Richards Garvey was a domestic helper. Although his parents were poor, they were not destitute for they owned land. Both parents provided a comfortable home and environment for young Marcus. His father was known to have a lot of books because he loved to read.

Perhaps it was from his father that he grew to love reading. Throughout his life, his love for reading never waned. Young Marcus seemed to have been very happy attending elementary school and growing up in St. Ann's Bay.

Marcus working in a printery

Marcus worked as a printer and became so good at his job in a short time that he eventually became a young foreman in the Government Printery in Kingston, Jamaica. He loved his work. For one so young he was quite articulate and spoke out on behalf of the workers and their rights. He even organized a strike among printers and for this he lost his job.

Garvey and His Travels

★ Some of the countries Marcus Garvey visited.

In 1910 Marcus Garvey travelled extensively through Central and South America, from Panama and most of Central America to Venezuela and Colombia in South America. He also visited most of the countries in the Caribbean.

In 1912 Garvey travelled to the United Kingdom and some countries in Europe, and in 1916 he travelled to the U.S.A. and Canada.

In 1910 Garvey began travelling through Central and South America. He first lived in Costa Rica because there he had an uncle. He worked as a timekeeper on a banana plantation. He also did some editing of local newspapers while in Costa Rica and Panama.

Throughout his travels in Central and South America he saw numerous Negro men working and living in awful conditions for very low wages. He tried unsuccessfully to help them. He even approached the British Consul to help but no help was forthcoming. The conditions under which black people were expected to live and work angered him for he knew that many West Indians had gone to these countries in search of work in order to better their lives. He also realized that many would die in these countries, never to return to their own homelands.

Garvey soon discovered that the large companies in these countries controlled much of the economy.

Because these companies had strong financial power and many were backed by some of the governments, they did as they liked. Garvey saw how powerless the black man was, but this did not deter him from the thought that all this could change if the people of colour (Negroes) around the world united for the good of the Negro race.

In his travels he began speaking to Negroes about the formation of their own government. He saw himself as the spokesperson for the Negro race and he felt that he should inform the black people of what the large fruit and sugar companies were doing.

Garvey returned to Jamaica in 1912 but was soon on his way to

England where he lived until 1914. While in England he attended Birbeck College where he studied philosophy and law. Sometimes he spoke at the famous Hyde Park Speaker's Corner. Because Garvey was an avid reader, it has been suggested that he came under the influence of thinkers such as Martin Delany, Henry McNeal Turner and Booker T. Washington. He read much of what they wrote and absorbed much of their philosophies.

Marcus Garvey believed that only if blacks were united could they be a feared, powerful force improving their condition. Garvey formed the Universal Negro Improvement Association (U.N.I.A.) and African Communities League (ACL) in 1914. The

Garvey observing workers on a banana plantation

motto of the Association was *"One God! One Aim! One Destiny!"* Its three main principles were:

- to unite the peoples of the West Indies, the negroes in the U.S.A. and Africans in Africa into one brotherhood for betterment and upliftment, and to set up a government for black people in Africa,

- to save Africa from further exploitation of its lands and labour,

- to achieve African nationalism – freedom for all black countries in Africa.

Marcus firmly felt that if black countries could become independent then they could develop their own aims and goals, and work toward these and their own destinies.

WHAT DID GARVEY PREACH?

- Self-reliance

- Black consciousness

- Racial pride

- Self-confidence

- Black unity

- Black dignity

- Black economic development

- Pan-Africanism

Marcus Garvey and The U.N.I.A.

The U.N.I.A. had branches all over the world. Garvey used this organization to spread his black consciousness philosophy and his ideas about Negro economic empowerment.

He published a weekly newspaper called *The Negro World*. In this newspaper which was circulated to many countries of the world, Garvey promoted his Pan-African philosophy.

The articles that were written in *The Negro World* showed Negroes in positive situations, situations that young Negroes could emulate. Marcus had many ideas. Filled with enthusiasm, he faced all challenges and thought himself to be the spokesman and the champion for all black people.

Black Star Line share certificate

The Black Star Line, a shipping line financed by Negroes, was incorporated and would transport goods between the U.S.A., the West Indies and Africa. The Black Star Line began operations in Delaware, U.S.A. June 23, 1919. Stocks

One of the ships of the Black Star Line

were sold for five dollars each. The shipping line would also transport African Americans back to Africa if they so wished. This Pan-African idea of Garvey became popular among Negroes.

The U.N.I.A. started certain businesses like the Universal Printing House, and the Negro Factories Corporation which was responsible for the building of many factories in the U.S.A. for the manufacturing of goods which were to be sold locally and for export. By the year 1920 this Negro Factories Corporation had established a variety of businesses sited in the United States of America. Many of these were operated as

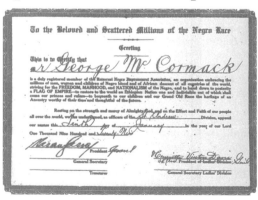

Membership card of the U.N.I.A.

cooperatives. About this time the U.N.I.A. had about 4 million members.

Marcus Mosiah Garvey was on a mission, building racial pride among black people. He kept calling for black dignity and black unity for he felt that only through unification of all black people could blacks (Negroes) prove that they could be the strong, powerful and progressive group which would improve their own position.

Marcus Garvey addressing thousands of workers in New York

The cry, "Up you mighty race, you can accomplish what you will", was the rallying cry for black people everywhere. Blacks were asked to give up mediocrity and negativity and start thinking positively, focusing on the good they had to offer, loving their race and respecting themselves.

In his own forceful and forthright way, Garvey tried to make black people aware that economic freedom for them would be had if they stood together, became self-reliant and controlled their own destiny. Garvey knew that most Negroes throughout the world felt inferior to whites primarily because they had been exposed to slavery and colonialism. Economic empowerment for Negroes was the answer. Garveyism became a strong, popular movement and was probably the largest and most powerful Negro Movement ever seen.

His message ran quickly throughout the world to black people everywhere. He became a hero to them. Of course, Garvey had many enemies, both white and black, inside his organization and outside of it. Some people saw him as a real threat. They were jealous of him and opposed his powerful ideas. Influential American Negroes felt intimidated by Garvey's thoughts and

philosophy and by the many millions of black people who by now had embraced Garveyism.

The Black Star Line stopped doing business and stopped sailing due to some serious difficulties the company faced. There was corruption and stealing by employees of the company, corruption by engineers and management and sabotage by the U.S.A. Bureau of Investigation. The purchase of used ships not reconditioned properly also contributed to the downfall of the Black Star Line. The company went bankrupt and Garvey was not able to repay the individuals who had invested in the company. They became disenchanted with him and turned away.

While in the United States, Garvey was persecuted and continuously investigated by individuals from the District Attorney's Office in New York but no proof of any crime was found.

However, after many persecutions, Garvey was eventually arrested and jailed in the U.S.A. after being charged and convicted of misusing the U.S.A. mail to defraud the American government. Many of Garvey's followers then and since have long thought that the charge was a trumped-up

Marcus Garvey being escorted to court by officials of the U.S. Justice system

A multitude of Jamaicans welcomed Garvey on his return to Jamaica

one. Why was there this fear of one individual? Why was he so persecuted? Why was the trial thought to be a one-sided affair? Garvey's supporters claimed that the trial was fraudulent. He was sentenced to five years in prison. His sentence was eventually commuted and he served nearly three years in jail. He was released in 1927 and sent back to Jamaica.

Garvey returned to Jamaica in 1927 to a very large welcome from the people of the island who showered him with love and praise. All along the streets leading to Liberty Hall excited onlookers packed the sidewalks just to get a glimpse of their champion. The atmosphere was like a carnival.

Garvey and Politics

Marcus Mosiah Garvey formed the People's Political Party (PPP) in 1929. It is said that this was the first modern Jamaican political party. It put out a manifesto and a list of the party's candidates.

Some important points of Marcus Garvey's PPP manifesto stated that there should be:

- an eight hour work day,

- a minimum wage,

- judicial integrity,

- land reform,

- a larger share of self-government,

- visiting health personnel for the rural poor,

- a legal aid department for the poor,

- technical schools for each parish,

- libraries and civic improvement for parish capitals,

- protection of native industries.

On one of the manifesto's points Garvey called for a law to imprison any judge who was found to be dealing unjustly with the people of the country. For this Garvey was arrested and charged with contempt of court and imprisoned for three months and fined £200 (two hundred pounds).

While Garvey was in prison he was elected councillor for the Allman Town Division of the Kingston & St. Andrew Corporation (KSAC). Because of his imprisonment he was not able to be present at the council meetings so he lost his seat.

After serving his time in prison, Garvey continued to campaign for seats in the then Legislative Council. His party was very popular and had a lot of supporters but was unable to do well because there was no Adult Suffrage at this time. Adult Suffrage only came about in 1944, allowing all citizens twenty-one and over the chance to vote.

Garvey did do some work for the KSAC. At one time he was elected unopposed to a seat in the council. Two men of his party, the PPP, also gained seats. All of his life Garvey was plagued with challenges, setbacks and harassments but these did not defeat him or deter him from his life's work which was getting the Negroes to have racial pride, become competent, to be self-confident, self-reliant and unified. He felt that Negroes should work for black economic independence and not rely on help from people of other races.

While in Jamaica Garvey kept organizing better working conditions and better pay for workers.

Marcus Garvey and Culture

Marcus Garvey and the U.N.I.A. developed different cultural forms for Jamaicans. A cultural centre called Edelweis Park in Kingston, was established by the Edelweis Amusement Company in 1931. When Jamaican artistes heard that an amusement company was set up to assist them to earn a living from what they did, they responded to the call. Artistes like Bim and Bam, Louise Bennett, Kid Harold, Ranny Williams, Ernest Cupidon and Arthur "Sagwa" Bennett were a few of those who performed at Edelweis. They eventually went on to become very famous performers.

Both Garvey and the U.N.I.A. believed in Jamaica and Jamaica's culture. There  was the firm commitment that all things Jamaican, professionally perfected, should be promoted locally and internationally.

Remembering Garvey

Garvey the orator and people's champion

Marcus Mosiah Garvey is internationally recognized. His beliefs have influenced many people and many popular leaders and groups around the world.

He has inspired many black individuals to cast off the shackles of mediocrity, negativity and incompetence, striving only for excellence. The Rastafarian movement of Jamaica is one religious group who sees him as a religious prophet.

Garvey left Jamaica for England in 1935 and continued his work there. He died in 1940 in London after suffering from poor health and two strokes. He was buried there.

In 1964 the Jamaican Government made him Jamaica's first National Hero. His remains were exhumed and returned to the island and laid to rest in the National Heroes' Park, Heroes' Circle, Kingston, Jamaica.

On August 17 each year, many countries of the world remember the Right Excellent Marcus Mosiah Garvey, entrepreneur, publisher, journalist, fiery orator, black nationalist and champion of black people throughout the world. He was the person who advocated the idea of Pan-Africanism and promoted black economic empowerment. He was a man before his time.

June 1965, the famous activist and leader of the American Civil Rights Movement Dr. Martin Luther King, Jr, visited Jamaica. He gave his now famous tribute to Garvey. He said, *"Garvey is the first*

man of colour to lead and develop a mass movement. He was the first man on a mass scale and level to give millions of Negroes a sense of dignity and destiny and make the Negro feel he was somebody."

Memorials honouring the Right Excellent Marcus Garvey are numerous and are to be found throughout the world. They come in many different forms:

• coins and notes with his

portrait on them,

- Marcus Garvey Day – celebrated in some countries,
- busts of Garvey,
- buildings, streets and highways named after him,
- cultural centres named after him,
- songs and poems that are dedicated to him, or that mention his name.

Jamaican $20 coin dedicated to the Right Excellent Marcus Garvey, National Hero

Statue of Marcus Garvey in St. Ann's Bay

Marcus Says ...

- "Up you mighty race! You can accomplish what you will."

- "Progress is the attraction that moves humanity."

- "Men who are in earnest are not afraid of consequences."

- "The whole world is run on bluff."

- "Liberate the minds of men and ultimately you will liberate the bodies of men."

- "Intelligence rules the world, ignorance carries the burden."

- "Chance has never yet satisfied the hope of a suffering people."

- "A man's bread and butter is only insured when he works for it."

- "Love your race: respect yourself."

- "Africa for Africans at home and abroad."

- "The black skin is not a badge of shame, but rather a glorious symbol of national greatness."

- "A people without the knowledge of their past history, origin and culture is like a tree without roots."

- "If you haven't confidence in self, you are twice defeated in the race of life. With confidence, you have won even before you have started."

- "If Europe is for the Europeans, then Africa is for the black people of the world."

- "Look for me in the whirlwind or the storm, look for me all around you, for with God's grace, I shall come and bring with me countless millions of black slaves who have died in America and the West Indies and the millions in Africa to aid you in the fight for Liberty, Freedom and Life. "

Things To Do

1. Why did Marcus Garvey become angry when he saw Negroes working in the fields in South and Central America?

2. In your own words, what was Garvey's philosophy?

3. What was the Harlem Renaissance?

4. Which other famous Jamaican was involved in the Harlem Renaissance?

5. What was Garvey's message to black people?

6. What does self-reliance mean?

7. Where is Liberty Hall located?

8. Why was this place called Liberty Hall?

9. Which is your favourite Garvey quotation and why?

10. Look up the following words in your dictionary. Use them in sentences of your own.

avid	edit	forthcoming
articulate	empower	liberate
colonialism	empowerment	incompetence
defraud	enthusiasm	inferior
disenchanted	environment	mediocrity
economy	exploitation	philosophy